EMPLOYABILITY WHAT?

A YOUNG PERSON'S GUIDE TO EMPLOYABILITY SKILLS AND STANDING OUT FROM THE CROWD

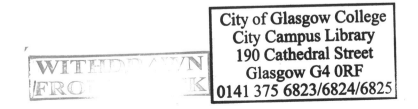

First published in the United Kingdom
in 2014 by
The Cloister House Press

ISBN 978-1-909465-23-7

Typeset and illustrated by
Lewis Alexander Jackson
www.lajackson.net

Acknowledgements

Without the incredible support and belief of my husband Allan and daughter Helena, this book would have remained a dream and for this I am eternally grateful.

The support of friends and family has been unbelievable too and with a list that could go on for a couple of pages, I'd like to particularly thank: my friend, mentor and boss Sam Whitaker; employability champions Stephen Logan and Kerrie Jaquest; true believer and supporter Kate Carroll; 'Action' Jackson for inspiring me and giving me the kick start I needed and my best friend Ruth Tremlett, a wonderful woman and amazing teacher who first told me I was on to something that could make a real difference.

Massive thanks also to my illustrator Lewis Jackson who has brought this book to life in a way I never thought possible and to Lydia Cox, a student who read my first draft and eventually gave me the feedback I needed to take this forward.

Contents

Introduction

Employability - that's all about work right?

Well yes but it starts way before you land your first job. In fact, developing your skills early may be the key to making you stand out from the crowd and get onto the careers ladder.

Whether you have your career mapped out and know what you need to do to get there or you are as yet undecided, making those first steps now is important.

It's also a good time to realise that formal qualifications are equally as important as personal skills so like it or not, you've got a lot of work to do!

This book will guide you through the seven key employability skills, why they are important and how to develop them. We'll also look at tools to help you get into the role you want, including advice on writing your CV and some interview tips you really need to know.

Employability v Enterprise

Before we start, it's worth just taking a minute to look at the difference between employability and enterprise.

You might have heard a lot about enterprise at school / college and be wondering if that means the same as employability. The truth of the matter is they are both different but one often depends on the other.

Enterprise or using your entrepreneurial skills is something that many employers like to see in their employees as this can help a business to grow and develop but many think of it as purely starting their own business and being their own boss, using a natural talent to spot an opportunity and run with it.

Employability on the other hand is more about the personal skills that mean you can get on with people and translate what you've learnt in the classroom into the world of work.

Whether you work for someone else or are destined to start your own business, you're going to need to understand and develop your employability skills.

In fact, if you're going to become an entrepreneur, your employability skills could mean the difference between having a successful business or not.

What are Employability Skills?

Putting it simply, employability skills are the basic personal skills and traits that any employer expects a potential new recruit to have. Of course formal qualifications are important but that's not all an employer looks at.

The seven key employability skills that have been defined by businesses in conjunction with the Confederation of British Industry are:

 Teamwork

 Self-management

 Business and Customer Awareness

 Application of Information Technology

 Application of Numeracy

Communication and Literacy

Problem Solving

Regardless of what stage you're at in your learning, it's well worth understanding what these skills are. Some may seem obvious and that's great but it's more likely to be the case that whilst you under-stand the principle, being able to demonstrate the skill is a little trickier.

Throughout the first half of this book, we'll take a look at each of these skills in turn in order to help you maximise your potential. Focussing on these skills now will make things much easier in the future.

 ## Teamwork

" What a great weekend!
Team work achieved this result
today & I really couldn't be happier.
Maybe miracles do happen #F1 "

Lewis Hamilton

Formula 1 driver, artist, singer, songwriter, musician

What does it mean?

This is probably the easiest skill to explain and understand. Putting it simply, this proves you can work as part of a group whether as 'one of the team' or in more of a leadership capacity.

Examples:

School sports team

Member of a band

10

But that doesn't apply to me…

Maybe so, but that doesn't mean you've never demonstrated your teamwork skills.

When it comes to being asked this question in an interview, many school or college leavers struggle to come up with an example. When you take the time to think about it, you work as part of a team more often than you may have thought.

Have you ever done a group enterprise activity? What about worked in pairs to do a school science experiment? You may even have taken part in a school production in recent years.

Examples aren't just limited to the classroom or sports pitch though, there's plenty of opportunity to hone your skills at home too. You may be a keen cook and like to help out in the kitchen or you might help out looking after younger siblings. These may not seem obvious but if you don't play your part as a member of the team, the team won't be effective and the job may not get done.

Try and come up with two examples of how you've demonstrated teamwork skills. You may also want to make a brief note about what you did as part of the team and if you achieved your goals. These notes will help you later in the book.

1. _____

_____

Notes:

_____

_____

_____

_____

2. _____

_____

Notes:

_____

_____

_____

_____

So why is it important?

There are times when independent working is right for your role but it's rare that you will ever work completely alone so an employer needs to know that you can work alongside others to get the job done.

It's common to have to work with people you may not know well so being practiced at working in different types of teams will help you when it comes to work and will prepare you for working alongside different personality types.

Jobs that require a lot of teamwork include:

Armed Forces

F1 Race Team

Manufacturing

Self-management

> " Ladies and gentlemen — it is done.
> MY ESSAY IS FINISHEDDDDDDDDDD!!!!
> #finally it's been a long day and
> now I have to train.. "

Hannah Crockroft MBE

Double Paralympic Gold Medallist, double world champion, 24x world record breaker. Hurricane Hannah, galaxy defender

What does it mean?

The skill of self-management might also be referred to as using your initiative. It means taking responsibility for yourself, your actions and for progress towards your targets.

Examples:

Training for a competition

Learning to play an instrument

But that doesn't apply to me...

OK, so these are extreme examples that might apply to only a handful of students but it's a pretty safe bet you demonstrate self-management every day without even realising it.

Do you complete you coursework and hand it in by the deadline? Do you (at least try to) get to school / college on time and in the correct uniform? Do you still have to be dragged out of bed in the morning or have you progressed to setting an alarm?

Believe it or not, each of these things demonstrates you have some level of self-management skills. As with many of the employability skills, we learn and develop them over time and it's easy to recognise that with self-management.

Think about it, we start off being fed meals that have been prepared for us and after some guidance and plenty of practice we can cook for ourselves and others, hopefully without burning the house down and maybe even managing to tidy up after ourselves and leave the kitchen as we found it.

Self-management is commonly described as coming through the following process:

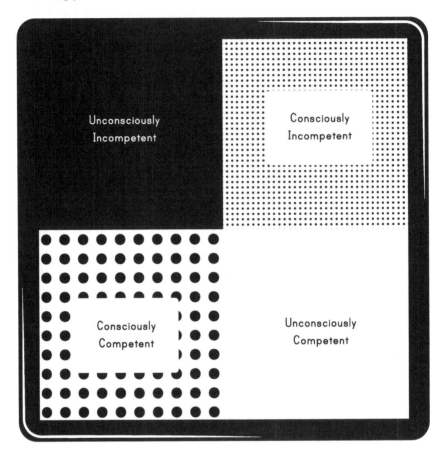

Or in other words: you don't know you can't do something because you're not aware of it – you know you can't do something – with training you now know what you're doing – the task is now second nature and you don't need to think about it as you do it.

Think of it like the process of learning to drive.

Try and come up with two examples of how you've demonstrated your self-management skills. You may also want to make a brief note about what you did and how it helped you reach your goals. These notes will help you later in the book.

1. _____

_____

Notes:

_____

_____

_____

_____

2. _____

_____

Notes:

_____

_____

_____

_____

So why is it important?

The world of work is a busy one and employers don't have the time to babysit new recruits.

Sure you'll receive training and support for whatever role you undertake but your future boss will need to know that you can not only make it to work on time but that you can complete the tasks asked of you.

Better still, they want to know you can show initiative and can spot when things need to be done.

Jobs that require a lot of self-management include:

HGV Driver

Hairdresser

Health Visitor

18

Business and Customer Awareness

" Half year review meeting tomorrow with the whole company. Important everyone understands key priorities for the business in H2 "

Phil Jones

MD at tech brand Brother UK aiming to inspire businesses and people by sharing leadership, technology and EQ insights

What does it mean?

It means simply that. Understanding different types of businesses, how their people work together and how they make money is the key to making a business successful.

Examples:

Raising money for charity or school / college funds

Work experience

lemonade for charity

But that doesn't apply to me...

This is the hardest skill to demonstrate whilst still in education and that's fine. Unless you are studying business, you might not start to develop this skill until you're in employment.

If you get the opportunity to go out on work experience, that's a great way to develop your business and customer awareness skills but if not, maybe you've taken part in something like the Young Enterprise Company Programme, which allows students to set up a trading business for a school year, or simply made and sold something to raise money.

If this is a particularly difficult skill for you to demonstrate, why not pick a company, perhaps the company you'd love to work for, and do your research. Find out about the company, what their vision is, what their product and market is and how they interact with their customers.

Try and come up with two examples of how you've demonstrated business and customer awareness skills. You might also want to make a brief note about what you did or what you learned. These notes will help you later in the book.

1. _____

_____

Notes:

_____

_____

_____

_____

2. _____

_____

Notes:

_____

_____

_____

21

So why is it important?

This skill is important in any industry but to give you an idea, let's use the leisure and tourism industry as an example.

A hotel relies on staff at all levels to understand how it's business works and where the customer fits in. If the check in service isn't friendly and efficient, if the rooms have not been cleaned to a decent standard or the food just isn't up to much, customers will let you know.

They may ask for their money back which of course is not good for business or they're more likely to share their bad experience with friends and family or even worse, with whoever wants to check out customer reviews on line.

Ever heard of the saying "The customer is always right"?

Jobs that require a lot of business and customer awareness include:

Entrepreneur

Call Centre Worker

Sales Assistant

Application of Information Technology

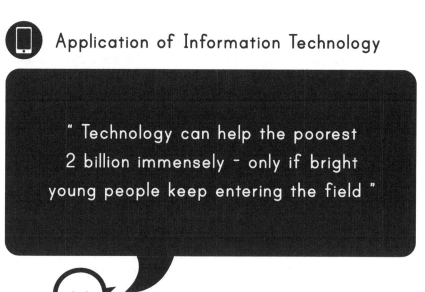

" Technology can help the poorest
2 billion immensely − only if bright
young people keep entering the field "

Bill Gates

Sharing things I'm learning through my foundation work and other interests...

What does it mean?

Application of information technology as a skill shows that you nderstand and can use effectively all manner of technology from knowing your way around a computer to more advanced forms of technology depending on the industry you go into.

Examples:

Coding

Writing a personal blog

But that doesn't apply to me...

You might be right. Coding may only be something done by a few and writing blogs isn't for everyone but unless you've been living under a stone, it's safe to say you can use some form of information technology.

Can you work your way around a computer, using the appropriate package for your coursework? Can you send an e-mail? Whether it's researching something for school / college or just searching for a bargain, it's safe to assume you can navigate your way around the internet. You probably even do it on the go now thanks to mobile phone technology.

For many young people, making the link between how technology is used whilst at home or school / college and how it's used in the workplace can be difficult. Fortunately, as you have been born into a generation that embraces and adapts to new technology so easily, it's very likely that your skills can be quickly be put to use in the workplace.

Try and come up with two examples of how you've demonstrated application of information technology skills. You might want to make a brief note about the different types of technology you used and the outcomes. These notes will help you later in the book.

1. _____

_____

Notes:

_____

_____

_____

_____

2. _____

_____

Notes:

_____

_____

_____

_____

So why is it important?

Over recent years business has and will continue to be incredibly IT focussed. From the computers used in every office across the country to the terminals used to calculate your bill in a restaurant or to check stock in another branch, information technology now defines how we do business and communicate so there's a very natural link between your communication and literacy skills and your application of information technology skills.

Many businesses use specialist software packages and there will always be training but an employer needs all new recruits to know the basics – the rest will follow soon enough and you're likely to continue to develop your skills throughout your career as technology continues to progress.

Jobs that require a lot of application of information technology include:

Web Developer

Graphic Designer

Purchasing Clerk

Application of Numeracy

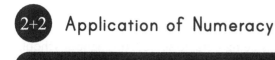

> " Swotting up on Christmas retail facts for my broadcast in the morn from @asda where 11million items are expected to be sold every hour. "

Steph McGovern

Business reporter @BBCBreakfast. Moonlight @BBC5Live @BBCRadio2 @BBCRadio4. Outside media world I'm a school governor + retired Irish dancer

What does it mean?

Application of numeracy is quite simply the ability to bring the maths you've learnt in the classroom into the workplace.

Examples:

School enterprise task

Design and technology project

But that doesn't apply to me...

Love it or hate it, with maths being a staple subject throughout school, you will certainly have some level of skill in this area.

There are many practical ways you may have been able to demonstrate the skill. Have you ever done a sponsored event to raise money for charity or school funds? Have you got your own bank account and save for what you want or do you know exactly what you want to buy with your birthday money? Even knowing what time the bus is that you need to catch and having the correct fare ready is a demonstration of your numeracy skills.

Ok, this may sound very basic and might need to be expanded on through the rest of your learning but the point here is that by understanding how you demonstrate this in daily life you can begin to expand on your skills.

Try and come up with two examples of how you've demonstrated application of numeracy skills. You might want to make a brief note about how this skill was applied and what the results were. These will help you later in the book.

1. _____

_____

Notes:

_____

_____

_____

_____

2. _____

_____

Notes:

_____

_____

_____

So why is it important?

Numeracy...numbers...money. Let's face it; no business can survive without this skill.

The obvious example here is retail, with every product having a cost price, a selling price and a profit margin. Whether you're responsible for setting these prices, ordering sufficient stock or making sure you give the right change at the till, an employee needs to be able to demonstrate this skill.

The business examples aren't just restricted to retail though so it's almost guaranteed that whatever industry you go into, you'll need to use, continually develop and apply your numeracy skills.

With application of numeracy, it easy to assume that what you're being taught in the classroom won't be used again after you've taken your exams but regardless of your career path, you'll certainly be using these skills in the future.

Jobs that require a lot of application of numeracy include:

Accountant

Quantity Surveyor

Chef

🍅	1
🫑	4
rice	2 1/2 cups
🍾	2 oz
🌰	100 g

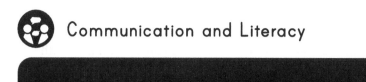

Communication and Literacy

" Technical theatre jobs require specific knowledge...The most important underlying skills are communication and collaboration "

American Theatre

The national magazine for the American Professional not-for-profit theatre

What does it mean?

The skill of communication and literacy looks at the spoken and written word and how you use them to interact with others in a business setting.

Examples:

Producing a school / college newspaper

Delivering a presentation or speech

But that doesn't apply to me...

Maybe not but there are dozens of examples you can come up with which form part of your daily life.

Most of what you do in lessons or coursework will be written – that's communicating your message in writing, hopefully with good use of English. If you've ever been part of a team, say a sports team in a PE lesson or working on a group task in class, you will have had to talk to each other to plan what you need to do next.

You will have been developing your communication and literacy skills for most of your life. The trick is being able to draw on those skills when it counts, like in an interview.

Try and come up with two examples of how you've demonstrated communication and literacy skills. You might want to make a brief note about the types of communication you used and whether it was successful. These will help you later in the book.

1. _____

_____

Notes:

_____

_____

_____

_____

2. _____

_____

Notes:

_____

_____

_____

_____

So why is it important?

No matter the industry, communication and literacy skills are of vital importance to every business. It doesn't matter if you're in the boardroom or at the sales counter, every person in business needs to be able to communicate. Face to face, internal communications, e-mails, letters, telephone or graphics, every bit of how you communicate sells the company's message.

As with all employability skills, you will develop your communication and literacy skills over time. A young person who is reluctant to be overheard making a business 'phone call at first may in all likelihood end up adding 'excellent telephone manner' to their CV in years to come. I know I did.

Jobs that require a lot of communication and literacy include:

Teacher

Doctor

Journalist

Problem Solving

> " When you start something new
> there is often a stubborn obstacle
> in the way. Think creatively
> & you'll get around it "

Richard Branson

Tie-loathing adventurer and thrill seeker who believes in turning ideas into reality. Acclaimed entrepreneur behind the Virgin brand.

What does it mean?

Does the term 'problem solving' really need explaining? It literally is about how well you can overcome a problem using the skills and resources at your disposal.

Examples:

Dealing with a conflict at school / college

Overcoming a personal difficulty

But that doesn't apply to me...

OK, think about the things you've done in school or college. Have you ever done a project or task where you've had to work to a specific brief that may have included a problem or two? You might even have some examples you hadn't thought of before from design and technology where you knew what the end product needed to look like and had to figure out a way of using your materials to get there.

Problem solving comes in many different forms, even if you can't think of anything obvious like an enterprise challenge, just finding a way to overcome a personal difficulty is demonstrating your problem solving skills. You might suffer with nerves or have a phobia of something in particular and have found a way to overcome it.

Often problem solving is put to the test at home as siblings don't always get on well and with all those hormones coming into play in your early teens, there are sure to be some family disagreements that you'll need to work together to overcome. It's just about how you learn from it in case you need to draw on those skills or experiences again.

Try and come up with two examples of how you've demonstrated problem solving skills. You might want to make a brief note about the problem and your solution. These will help you later in the book.

1. _____

_____

Notes:

_____

_____

_____

_____

2. _____

_____

Notes:

_____

_____

_____

_____

So why is it important?

Problem solving skills are used a lot in business, so much so that you will eventually get used to dealing with the smaller scale problems without even realising it. Think about a complaining customer – before long you'll have learnt and developed techniques to deal with them until doing so becomes second nature. That's exactly what employers need.

It's not just about dealing with customers though, employers need staff who can deal with what is thrown at them and who can find and implement a successful solution.

Jobs that involve a lot of problem solving skills include:

Project Manager

Lawyer

Customer Care Assistant

Combining Employability Skills

Now we've looked at each of the employability skills individually, you will hopefully start to recognise times where more than one skill would need to be used.

Think about these situations:

You are working on an experiment with a partner in science but can't agree on the best method to use.

To complete this task you will need to use:

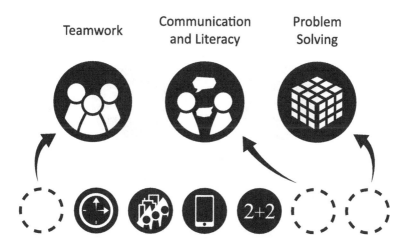

Let's look at this a little closer...

The fact that you can't agree on the best method indicates that there's a problem. You are working with a partner, which let's face it, means you're part of a small team. Hopefully by talking the problem through (communicating) or even sketching out how you think it should be done you'll be able to work out a solution together.

Can you start to see how easy it is to demonstrate your skills?

You have decided to do a sponsored event with a couple of friends to raise money for a local charity.

To complete this task you will need to use:

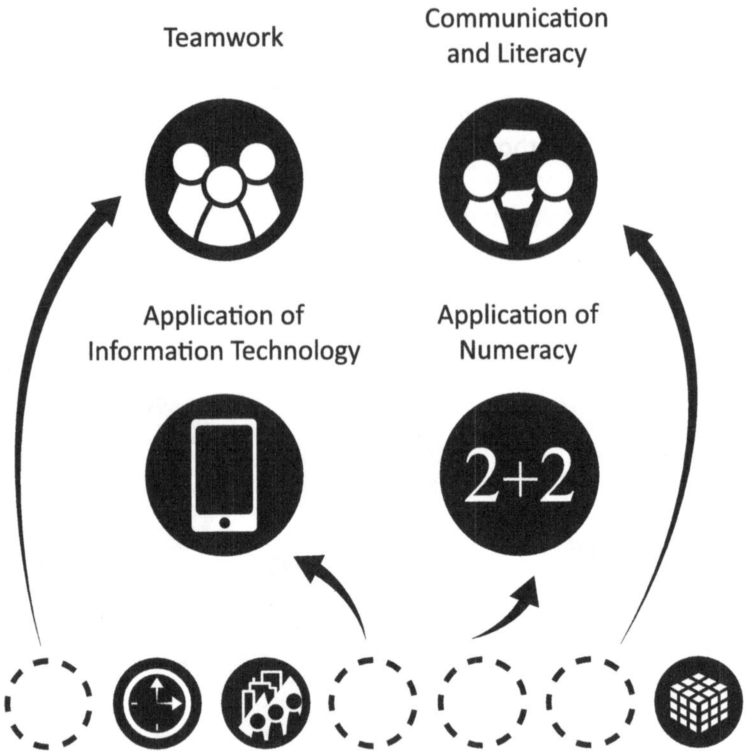

Teamwork

Communication and Literacy

Application of Information Technology

Application of Numeracy

2+2

Let's look at this a little closer...

You're working with a couple of friends – this straight away means you're working as part of a team and are communicating with each other to plan out what you are going to do. You might be telling others what you're doing by using posters or sending e-mails to ask for sponsorship so that's you're communication and literacy covered.

If you're doing a sponsored event then by definition you'll be dealing with money in some form or another so that means you'll be using your application of numeracy skills. If you've decided to collect your sponsorship by setting up an on-line sponsor page then you're also demonstrating your application of information technology skills.

You have exams in several subjects coming up and need to revise for them.

To complete this task you will need to use:

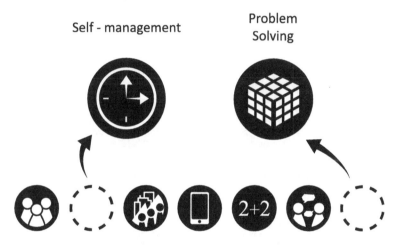

Self - management

Problem Solving

Let's look at this a little closer...

You might not think you're demonstrating any employability skills here but this is a really good example to draw on in an interview.

When exams come round, it's often during one particular period in the year and this means revision for lots of different subjects at the same time. We won't go in to the various different techniques for doing this but suffice to say you will need to decide how you go about revising and prioritising your revision. More importantly, you'll need to be strict with your time and make sure you're not being distracted which is a great example of how you use your self-management skills.

Once you understand how these skills are combined and used in school / college, you can start to see how they would be used in the world of work.

Here are a few examples from different sectors:

A client of the marketing company you are working for wants a digital archive of their work.

To complete this task you will need to use:

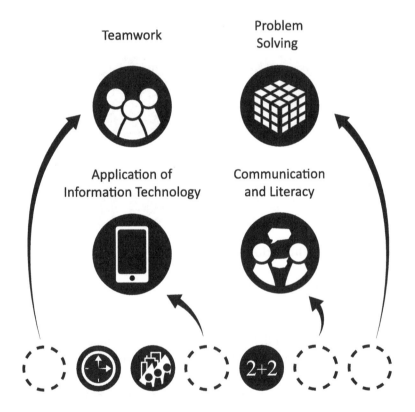

Teamwork

Problem Solving

Application of Information Technology

Communication and Literacy

Let's look at this a little closer...

The word 'digital' should have given you the idea from the start that you'll need to use your application of information technology skills to deliver this for the client.

You'll need to demonstrate your problem solving skills by working out how you can deliver what your customer wants by using the resources and technology at your disposal.

In a busy marketing company, it's unlikely that you'll be responsible for every step in the process meaning that you'll need to demonstrate both your communication and literacy skills and your teamwork skills as you work with your colleagues to deliver what your customer wants.

A customer at the clothing store you are working at has asked for a discount for a damaged item.

To deal with this task you will need to use:

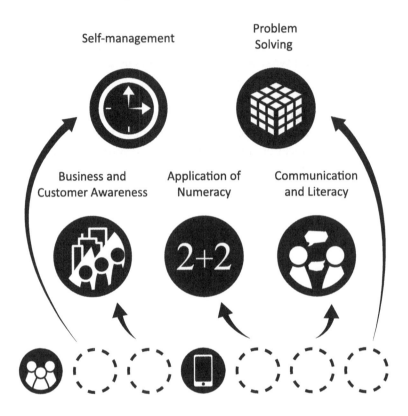

Let's look at this a little closer...

The first step in dealing with a situation like this is always to exercise some self-management. If the customer remains calm then it's easier for you to do the same but as soon as a customer begins to get a little more animated or abusive, it's important to keep a cool head.

The next big skill in this situation is business and customer awareness and it's easy to think that the part you're focussing on is around the customer. In actual fact, the area you really need to focus on is that of your business. You'll need to know what the policy on this is, what flexibility you have in this situation, who you need to call on for help and what you might need to let the customer know about returning the item. This is also the perfect example of your problem solving skills as you find the right solution to the situation which will mean the customer is happy and the business has not suffered a loss.

By knowing what discount you can give to your customer and being able to successfully give the refund, you'll have put your application of numeracy skills to good use and by simply speaking to the customer and any colleagues you need to, you'll also be demonstrating your communication and literacy skills.

It's important to realise that whilst it might seem that this is a difficult situation to deal with, by using your employability skills you'll adapt to the situation and develop ways of dealing with it so that when it happens in the future, dealing with it just becomes second nature. When you're handling a situation like this seamlessly, you can begin to expand on the skills you're already using.

You work for a haulage company where your HGV drivers have their hours restricted by law. One of your drivers is going to run out of hours before being able to make a delivery of fresh food.

To deal with this task you will need to use:

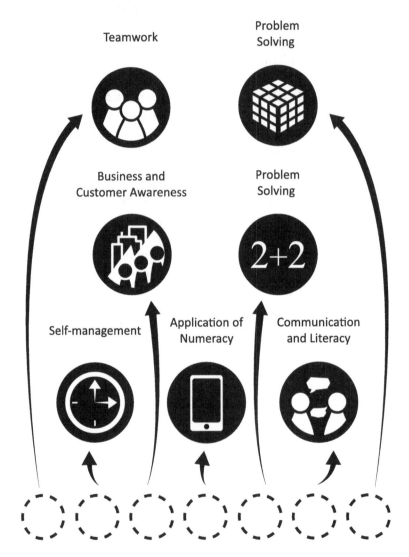

Teamwork

Problem Solving

Business and Customer Awareness

Problem Solving

Self-management

Application of Numeracy

Communication and Literacy

Let's look at this a little closer...

This challenge is going to test all of your skills and you'll have to find a solution quickly. The first step is to know your business and your customer – do you have a standard procedure for when this happens as it's not going to be the first time the business has encountered this problem. It's important to also understand the customer's needs as a delay in your delivery could have huge knock on effects.

Even if there is a standard way of dealing with this, your problem solving skills are still going to be put to the test and it will be down to you to use your application of numeracy skills to calculate hours of other drivers, fuel, fines etc. Your application of information technology will also come into play as you use vehicle tracking systems and the like to find the solution.

Now unless you're going to go and meet your stranded driver and take the delivery yourself, you're going to need to call on your teamwork skills as you work with other drivers and colleagues to rearrange the delivery.

You might not realise that self-management comes into play in this situation but it really does. There are times when you need to drop everything to deal with an important or time critical task like this. If the delivery is due in two hours but it's your lunch time, you might just have to take a later lunch and deal with the problem first.

Communication and literacy runs all the way through this challenge from taking that first call from your driver to speaking to the customer and your colleagues.

Now we've looked at the skills needed by employers, we'll look at some practical advice, hints and tips to help you feel confident in preparing yourself for the world of work.

Experience, Experience, Experience

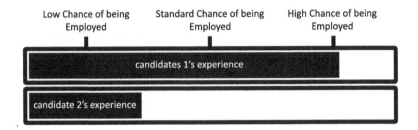

Many adults you speak to will tell you that it's easier to get a job when you already have one. That doesn't have to be the case if you take any opportunity you can to gain experience and test out your employability skills.

One of the best ways to do this is through work experience which is normally done during the last couple of years of school or a more specific work placement if it's appropriate to a college course.

Before it's time to go out on work experience, it's a good idea to have a think about the kind of career you'd like. Due to things like data protection or health and safety it may not be possible to get the exact placement you'd like but your school / college will always do their best to find the right fit.

If you have a company in mind that you'd like to work for, there's nothing wrong with approaching them yourself and if they agree, passing their details to your work experience co-ordinator to carry out the necessary checks.

If you don't know what career you want in the future then don't worry, there are many students your age (and many adults who have been working for years) who aren't completely sure what they want to do yet. The important thing is to take the opportunity to gain some experience.

Top tips before your placement

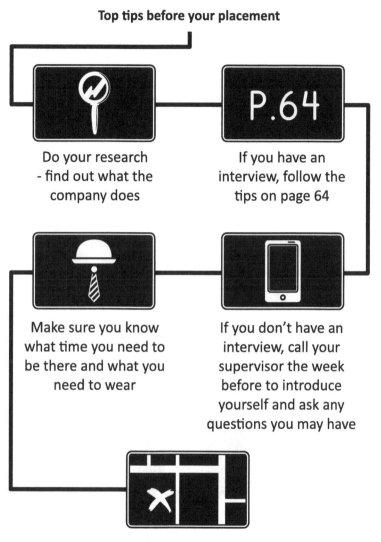

Do your research - find out what the company does

If you have an interview, follow the tips on page 64

Make sure you know what time you need to be there and what you need to wear

If you don't have an interview, call your supervisor the week before to introduce yourself and ask any questions you may have

Make sure you know exactly where the building is and how you'll get there - a trial run is always sensible

Top tips whilst you're on your placement

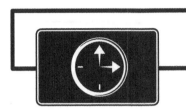

Make sure you arrive on time

Don't be afraid to ask questions or for things to be repeated

Find out about how your colleagues got into their roles

If you run out of work, ask for more don't just sit and wait for someone to notice

Keep a journal or diary about what you did in your role and the employability skills you demonstrated. This will help you update your CV

Whether you do work experience through school / college or not, there are other ways to gain some experience whilst you're still in education. Weekend or holiday jobs are ideal but in the majority of industries you will need to wait until you're 16 for this but you can certainly get some experience by starting at the bottom of the ladder. I bet almost every hairdresser started by sweeping the floors and washing hair on a Saturday.

Another way to gain experience and practice your employability skills is through volunteering. You might already have a charity you want to work with but if not, check out who is in your local area. From helping out at an animal shelter to doing something to raise funds or even helping to support a local race as a marshal, charities are always in need of volunteers. It looks great on your CV too.

If you've done work experience or even something like babysitting or a newspaper round, make a brief note about it here. Don't forget to cover what you did and the skills you used. Try to come up with two good examples.

1. _____

_____

Notes:

_____

_____

_____

_____

2. _____

_____

Notes:

_____

_____

_____

_____

Your Next Step

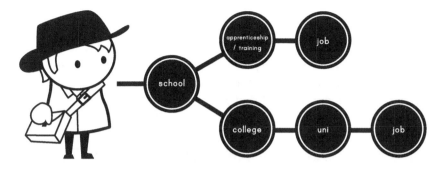

With all this talk of employability skills and the world of work you may be trying to figure out what your next step will be. With recent generations that choice was often simple – if you were academically minded you went from school to college to university and finally into work in a professional position or you would go straight into work after school, often doing a more practical role.

The good news is that your next step is completely up to you.

The school – college – university route may be perfect for you and that's great but it doesn't suit everyone. Likewise getting straight into a job when you leave education (either school or college) might or might not be the right choice for you.

Thankfully, as your careers advisor will be able to tell you, there are many different routes that are now open to you. Thanks to apprenticeships and part time degrees, it's possible to combine your further learning with practical, on the job training which allows you to get a head start on putting your employability skills into practice and earning whilst you do so.

If you know what your route is going to be, why not make a note of it here? This is for no other reason than to make you think about where you want to get to and how you're going to do it.

If you don't know the route you're going to take, this will act as a prompt to do your research and to look at your options.

Even if you don't know what career you want to end up in, you can still make some notes on some possible routes you may want to follow. If you definitely know university isn't for you, your notes may be as simple as: "I want to do an apprenticeship but I'm not sure what in." You've then got your prompt that your next step is to do some research on the huge array of different apprenticeships available.

The career I want	The route I want to take

The rest of this book focusses on your CV and the interview process – something you will need to work on if you're venturing into the world of work on a full time basis or simply finding a part time job to support you in your studies.

Standing Out from the Crowd

So we've looked at each of the employability skills and how important they are. We've also looked at how to start to fine tune your skills through experience but what happens next?

Chances are that most of your fellow students will be in the same position as you so what you need to do is simple. You need to stand out from the crowd.

Following the advice in this book is no guarantee you'll go out and land your dream job but it's a good place to start. And so is this particular piece of advice.

When a business advertises a job it's a fairly safe bet they'll receive a raft of almost identical looking CVs that they'll need to filter through, usually by looking at the qualifications and most recent experience first.

So how do you stand out from the crowd and make sure that your CV is one that gets noticed? Well the real answer is that that's up to you. It might be as simple as following the advice on getting some practical experience by volunteering. A write up on what you did and the skills you used is a good indication to a potential employer that you have good self-management skills.

What about looking at things a little differently though?

We'll talk a lot more about your CV in a later section but here's something to think about... there's no law to say that all CVs must be on plain white paper devoid of anything that would make it personalised to you?

Of course it may not be appropriate for everyone but if you want a career in graphic design, why not do something eye-catching? If you want to be a journalist why not make your CV look like a newspaper clipping?

At the very least, why not use a different colour paper or send it in a brightly coloured envelope?

It's not all about how you present your CV though; delivery is a big part too. If you're able to, dress smartly and go and hand deliver your CV and covering letter. It's always good if you can hand it over to the right person as its ideal for getting them to remember you. Think about it, a well presented CV handed over to the named contact in a brightly coloured envelope is already making you stand out when compared to the pile of plain and ordinary letters on their desk. If you're just handing out your CV on the off chance a company may have a position, this is also a good way to go about it.

If you've sent your CV through the post, even something as simple as calling two or three days later to make sure it was received might make them pull it out of the pile and take a closer look.

Writing the Perfect CV

So what is a CV? Well, to give it it's full name, a curriculum vitae is a document which tells a potential employer all about your qualifications and experience, preferably in no more than a couple of pages.

There is no right way to write a CV but the template we are going to look at contains the information businesses want to see.

The first thing to remember when it comes to writing your CV is that you are creating an advertisement for yourself and only with successful advertising will someone want to go to the next step and want to meet you at an interview.

A perfect example of this is making sure that there are no grammar or spelling errors in your finished document – no-one will want to interview someone who can't be bothered to take the time (or ask for support) to check their CV and correct any errors.

The next big thing to remember is never to lie on your CV. By adding in skills or experience you don't actually have you are sure to be found out when it comes to the interview stage or worse, when you land the job but can't do the tasks asked of you.

Hopefully you have been filling in the notes sections throughout this book and we'll start to look at how we can include this information in your CV.

So let's have a look at an ideal format...

Name and contact details

Your CV should always start with your name clearly shown at the top of the page along with all of your contact details. If you're going to add an e-mail address, make sure it's one you check regularly. It might also be a good idea to make sure it's an appropriate e-mail address to be given out to a business rather than a joke or nickname one.

Personal Profile

Think of this as the 'About Me' section. This section, usually about a paragraph long, will often be the thing that will make an employer want to read on or not. This is where you will write from a business perspective about the things you enjoy and that you feel are your strengths. Try not to use too many negative words when writing about yourself as this can make you come across as stubborn or inflexible.

Don't be worried if this section is the most difficult to write and you have to keep coming back to it, it's perfectly normal to find it difficult to talk about and promote yourself but in this process, that's something you need to try and work on.

Some of your notes will help you here so think about incorporating one or two of your employability skills notes from the earlier pages and draw particular attention to them by giving basic examples such as "I enjoy the challenge of working as part of a team and have put my teamwork skills to good use through various enterprise activities in school". This is instantly telling an employer that you can function as part of a team and have experience doing so.

Education and Qualifications

In this section you need to list (with the most recent first) the school and college you attended, when you attended and the qualifications you achieved. If your grades are predicted then make sure that's clear.

After your formal educational qualifications, you can add any other qualifications or grades you feel are appropriate. Dance, sport or music grades are great examples of your self-management and teamwork skills but these are the kind of things that can be removed from your CV as time goes on and you gain qualifications more in line with your career.

Employment and Experience

Your previous employment and experience should be shown starting with the most recent first. Each job should be treated as a separate paragraph and should start with the organisation you worked for, your job title and your start and finish dates (month and year is fine).

For each role you need to summarise what your responsibilities were and any particular accomplishments you had in the role. Try to find a balance here so you avoid listing out every one of your duties. Your notes from the earlier section on experience (page 52) will help you to complete this section.

Don't be worried if you are at the stage of going for your first full or part time role and don't have a previous 'job' to write about. Make sure you include your work experience and you can also add any appropriate things from school or college as long as you can draw skills and experience from them. For example: "As part of our Business Studies course we took part in the Young Enterprise Company Programme which saw me take on the position of Marketing Manager for our business which successfully made and sold bespoke cushions over the course of a school year"

Hobbies and Interests

Outside of work, your hobbies and interests make you who you are so in this section you should aim to include any clubs you belong to, any sporting activities, anything you are learning outside of school / college and anything you simply enjoy. Bear in mind that whilst it's great to say you enjoy socialising with friends, many others will say the same so it's important you look to put something here that will make you stand out.

From an employer's perspective, this is the area within your CV that will show who you really are as a person. It might be that you have a particular skill or interest that could open up doors for you by highlighting something that neither of you had considered. For example, by noting that you are a keen amateur photographer, an employer might spot an opportunity for you to put your skills to work in helping to promote their products or services.

References

When you're in employment and looking for another position it may not be appropriate to put your current employer's details as a reference so it's perfectly acceptable to say that your references are available on request as these wouldn't normally be sought until after the interview stage which would allow you the opportunity to talk about your current position.

At this stage in your career, the most likely references will be from your work experience placement and from a teacher. First and foremost, you need to ask for their permission to use them as a reference so they are not put on the spot when a potential employer calls. It's also sensible to double check with them what contact details they want giving out as some may prefer phone to e-mail or vice versa.
It might even be worth asking your work experience provider or your teacher if they would be prepared to write a reference for you so that should you get to the interview stage, you can take it in with you.

So now we've talked about a CV, let's have a look at an example. Had I have known what I know now about writing a CV, this is how mine would have looked at age 16 having recently left school.

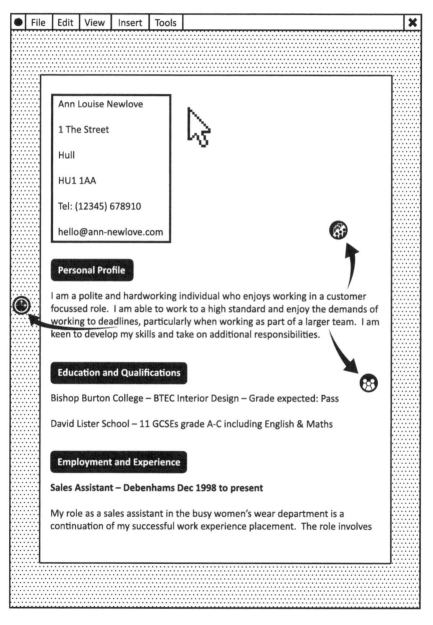

working as part of a busy team to ensure that the department is well stocked and tidy.

Work Experience – Debenhams October 1998

During my two weeks work experience at the busy department store, my work experience was split across two departments; merchandising and shop floor. Whilst working with the merchandising department, I worked different hours to ensure that any display changes were completed before the store opened to minimise disruption. The role also involved updating window displays, re-painting an area when a designer's branding changed and preparing items ready for the Christmas displays.

Whilst on the shop floor, I worked on the women's wear department where I assisted with putting out new stock, housekeeping, wrapping at the till point and returning unwanted items from the fitting room. I enjoyed both weeks of my work experience and found that I preferred interacting with the customers and helping to fulfil their needs.

Saturday Sales Assistant – The Landscape Centre March 1996 – October 1998

The Landscape Centre was a family business and I helped out on a Saturday and during the summer holidays. My roles included watering plants, looking after the animals in the pet area and serving customers. I also assisted with putting together seasonal displays and was trained to make Christmas Wreaths and hanging baskets to customer's orders.

Hobbies and Interests

I am very interested in interior design and like to make and refurbish things at home, in particular using textiles. I enjoy baking and have done so from an early age. I'm also an active member of the Youth Association of Methodist Churches and hold the position of Secretary of the Yorkshire & Humber Area.

References

Available on request

Much of my CV was made up using my own notes in each of the employability skills sections and by picking out where the wording used is demonstrating my employability skills, you will hopefully start to understand how a potential employer reads a CV and the assumptions they are able to make from it.

Once you've created your CV, make sure you keep it up to date. This document, in one form or another, is going to be with you for the rest of your working life. Even if you land the perfect job straight away and stay there for many years, your skills and probably your role will continue to evolve. Set a six monthly reminder to have a look at your CV and see if it needs updating. It might just be that your language has become more sophisticated or technical due to the industry you have chosen or you might have done a course recently – either way, don't let it be forgotten about until the next time you come to look for a new job.

Interview Top Tips

Employability skills understood... CV prepared and delivered...fingers crossed the next stage is an interview.

From business feedback, regardless of how much effort you've put in to get to this point, an interview is where a young person comes up against the biggest problem yet. Nerves. This means that even if you know everything there is to know about employability skills, being able to give real and honest examples in an interview may be difficult.

If you get the opportunity to take part in a mock interview at school / college, that's a great way to get your first experience of an interview situation.

Everyone feels nervous in an interview and that's perfectly natural but how you handle those nerves may be key to landing a role. Don't forget, once you get to the interview stage, you've already successfully sold yourself through your CV and its now down to how your personality and skills come across when compared to the other candidates.

Depending on the organisation you may have a one to one interview or you may have an interview panel, usually consisting of the immediate line manager, a representative from the Human Resources department and anyone else who might need to be involved.

Follow these interview top tips to give you a helping hand and hopefully settle those nerves:

Before the interview

Make sure you know where you're going. Have a trial run the day before

Do your research on the company and make a note of your questions

Dress appropriately - it doesn't have to be a business suit if it's not right for the position but you still need to be smart

Gather any necessary documents such as a portfolio of work if appropriate

Another top tip is to prepare your answers to some of the more common interview questions such as:

An example of when you've had to manage conflict - check your notes from the Problem Solving section

An example of how you have worked as part of a team - check your notes from the Teamwork section

An example of how you've had to manage your time - check your notes from the Self-management section

You don't need to recite these in the interview but by reading them before hand or if you're really nervous taking it in with you as a reminder will avoid you struggling to remember an example when you're put on the spot.

At the interview

Do

 Make sure you arrive on time

 Take a moment to breathe deeply to calm your nerves before going in

 Remember to turn your phone off

 Shake hands with the interviewer

 Answer your interviewer's questions honestly

 Listen carefully

Ask for a question to be repeated or re-phrased if you didn't hear it properly

 Ask questions - you should have prepared several questions before the interview

 Make one or two notes if appropriate

Thank the interviewer for their time

Don't

 Be late

 Chew

 Fidget

 Use bad language or slang

 Mumble

 Wear excessive jewellery or make-up - personality is fine but don't go overboard

 Go to far off topic - you're likely to be nervous but you'll need to stay on subject when answering questions

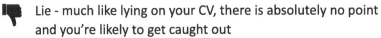 Lie - much like lying on your CV, there is absolutely no point and you're likely to get caught out

 Leave without asking any questions

Forget to ask what the next stage of the process is and when you are likely to hear back - remember not to appear pushy though

When you leave the interview, take some time to reflect on how it went. It might be your first interview, it might be your tenth but each and every one will be different and will allow you to improve your interview technique.

If you were particularly nervous and you felt that affected your performance, you might need to look at some coping strategies to help you.

If you ran out of questions to ask because they were answered naturally through the conversation, next time try to look a bit closer at the company's website before you go in. If you find that they do a lot for charity or in the local community, why not ask if there would be an opportunity for you to get involved should you be successful.

This show's that you've really done your research and could make you stand out from other candidates.

What happens next is again down to the organisation interviewing you. They may be able to let you know quickly whether or not you've been successful or there may be a longer process to follow. If you go past the point they said you would find out, there is no harm in a polite phone call to check if any decision has been made.

Continual Development

Once you've got that first job there's no telling where your career might take you. You might go straight into the field you always dreamed of and work your way up the ladder or you may be unsure where you want to be.

If you ask most adults they'll tell you they have taken the odd side step or are not in the field they thought they would be. They are also sure to tell you that they have learnt new skills and probably a lot about themselves in the process.

You might not appreciate it at this stage but you're likely to further your learning a lot through on the job training or similar. That doesn't have to be further or higher education but could be as simple as taking first aid training and becoming one of the nominated first aiders in your workplace. Just think of the use of your employability skills in that scenario and how that will look on your CV as you progress through your career.

You're actually likely to do more learning once you're in employment than through secondary school / college and it's important to keep on learning to keep your skills up to date and keep you competitive in the job market. Make sure you remember to add it to your CV too.

Whilst additional learning is important, so is continual personal development. This is all about making you a more confident person with rounded skills and knowledge.

Your employer will help you with your skills relating to your job but there's plenty you can do personally too. For example, there's a saying that 'people who present get promoted' so how about finding opportunities to present to your peers?

For me, the thought of speaking up, even in meetings, used to make me want to run from the room but having found that I had a problem and needed to address it, I started by chairing basic meetings with people I knew well and with a lot of nerve battling, ended up facing my fears and presenting at an event. I now happily volunteer to do talks to groups and am pleased with my progress in this area over the last couple of years. I've now got a great skill that I can call on when it's needed too.

There is a whole host of part time courses that you could put yourself through as well which could give you the confidence to try something new or to take one of those sideways steps in your career that we talked about earlier.

Another great way to develop yourself is to find a suitable mentor. Many schools and colleges now have mentoring schemes in place but it's a good idea to find your own too.

There are several ways you can go about finding a mentor such as:

•   Finding a mentor you may never actually meet but who you admire as a person for what they may have overcome, achieved, established or what they stand for and trying to put it into practice in your own life. Many entrepreneurs will say Sir Richard Branson is a mentor who they are likely never to meet in person

- Finding a mentor who is successful in your chosen field, possibly with a major national or international firm, who you may be able to form a mentor / mentee relationship with to help you develop in your professional career. This may be someone whose footsteps you would like to follow in and who may agree to meet you once or twice a year

- Finding a mentor who is successful in your chosen field, on a more local level, who you may be able to form a closer mentor / mentee relationship with to help you develop professionally and socially. This may be someone you can meet up with or communicate with on a more regular basis and who can help you with career advice. They may even be able to open up their networks to you and have opportunities within their own businesses that would be suitable for you

What happens in your career is down to you, to the opportunities you seize and to the connections you make. You can be whoever you want to be and can do anything you set your mind to doing so make sure you get a head start by developing your employability skills and putting them into practice early.

About the Author

Do you remember in the CV section that I said writing about yourself is one of the hardest things to do? Well here goes...

I'm now a wife and mum with a very busy work life but it hasn't always been like that. My teenage years weren't brilliant and due to illness I was almost unable to sit my GCSEs but thankfully I did and what's more, considering my school wasn't doing well at all in the league tables, I did pretty well. As you'll have seen from my CV, when I was younger I was positive I'd have a career in interior design but part way through college, things turned out a little differently for me. I did finish the course but then found myself taking a different route, working my way up the ladder in a number of small marketing and import companies before being made redundant and wondering what my next step would be.

My next step turned out to be the start of something very interesting indeed as I worked on delivering Hull's Building School for the Future programme and delivering on our legacy promises by helping to support young people in the area to increase their attainment and aspirations – it wasn't just all about the new buildings.

The role has opened up a great many opportunities for me and in addition to writing and the day job, I now provide the day to day management for the Employability Charter, a Humber-wide initiative bringing business and education together to develop the employability skills of young people. I'm an associate of the Institute of Employability Professionals and chair of a Career Academy Local Advisory Board at one of our Hull Building Schools for the Future schemes.

I'm not entirely sure how I fit everything in but I'm also pleased to sit on the board of Business Springboard, a local group set up to allow the next generation of business professionals to work together and develop the personal skills and networks that will help them get further in their careers.

A few years ago I wouldn't have been able to tell you what employability skills were, it just felt like plain old common sense but in working closely with many businesses and schools in the last few years, I came to realise how important these skills are and how difficult it was for young people to recognise and demonstrate them. In writing this book I wanted to show you that by thinking about how you approach things a little differently and by making the most of the opportunities you have in front of you, it really doesn't have to be that difficult.

Life is a journey; be prepared and make the most of it.

photo taken by @photomoments

Lightning Source UK Ltd.
Milton Keynes UK
UKOW06f1514050616

275645UK00004B/7/P